WORLD OF KNOWLEDGE
EXPLORERS

BELITHA PRESS

This edition published in 2003 by
Belitha Press
A member of Chrysalis Books plc
64 Brewery Road, London N7 9NT

Typeset by Chambers Wallace, London
Printed in China
British Library Cataloguing in Publication Data
for this book is available from the British Library.

ISBN 184138 602 2

Acknowledgements

Photographic credits:

Bryan and Cherry Alexander 25 bottom
The Bodleian Library 24
Christian Bonington 59 top
Bridgeman Art Library 21 top
John Cleare/Mountain Camera 9, 13 top, 32/33, 49 left, 51, 54 right, 55 centre
ET Archive 22, 23, 25 top left and right, 50 right
Mary Evans Picture Library 53 bottom, 54 left
Derek Fordham/Arctic Camera 57
Werner Forman Archive 15 bottom
Giraudon 27
Susan Griggs/Leon Schadeberg 6, /Victor Englebert 41 top, /Robert Azzi 46, /Anthony Howarth 47 top
Sonia Halliday 6 bottom
Robert Harding Picture Library 17, /George Douglass Brewerton: Crossing the Rocky Mountains, in the collection of The Corcoran Gallery of Art, Gift of William Wilson Corcoran 29, /Schloss Tegel, East Berlin 37 top, 44, 53 top
Michael Holford 14 left, 18 right, 35 top
Hulton Picture Company 21 bottom, 30, 37 bottom, 45 bottom
Hutchison Library 31 top, 41 bottom, 43
MacDonald/Aldus Archive 39, 42, 45 top
Magnum 32
Mansell Collection 33, 40, 50 left
Marion and Tony Morrison 34, 35 bottom, 36, 38
National Maritime Museum 14 right
Oxford Scientific Films 13 bottom, 19, 31 bottom
Photo Library of Australia 49 top
Popperfoto 47 bottom
Rapho 5
Ronan Picture Library 18 left
Science Photo Library 58
Frank Spooner Pictures 59 centre
Charles Swithinbank 55 top
Viking Museum, Oslo 10

Maps by: Lovell Johns Ltd
Illustrated by: Nick Shewring (Garden Studios), Eugene Fleury

Series editors: Neil Champion and Mark Sachner
Educational consultant: Carolyn Kain
Editors: Kate Scarborough and Rita Reitci
Designed by: Groom and Pickerill
Picture research: Ann Usborne

Contents

Words found in **bold** are explained in the glossary on pages 60 and 61

Early Explorers

CHAPTER ONE

WHY EXPLORE?

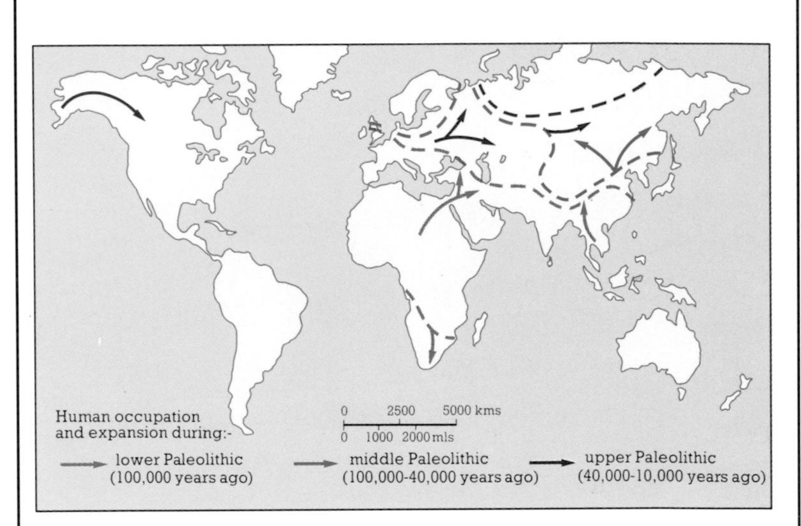

► This map shows how early people spread across the Earth (100,000 to 10,000 years ago).

▲ A group of Stone Age people, near the end of the last ice age (11,000 years ago).

What is Exploration?

About one million years ago some humans moved from regions of Africa to the cooler parts of the world. By the end of the last ice age, 11,000 years ago, people had spread to every **continent** except Antarctica. These early humans moved around, looking for better places to live. Explorers are different. They explore to find places to trade with, to steal, to learn, to become famous, to settle, or to spread religion. But all explorers have one thing in common. They want to bring or send knowledge of unknown places back to their homelands.

Growing nations

Explorers usually came from wealthy, growing nations. Some explorers were traders who wanted valuable metals, spices, or gems. While others were interested in what was beyond the horizon, or they were scholars who wanted to know more about other peoples, places, and ideas. Most of these explorers took great risks and found their journeys very difficult.

▲ These paintings of bison are on the walls of caves in Lascaux, France. The pictures are about 30,000 years old, made by people known as the Cro-Magnons.

▼ The people below lived for thousands of years before they first met with white European explorers.

The Greeks

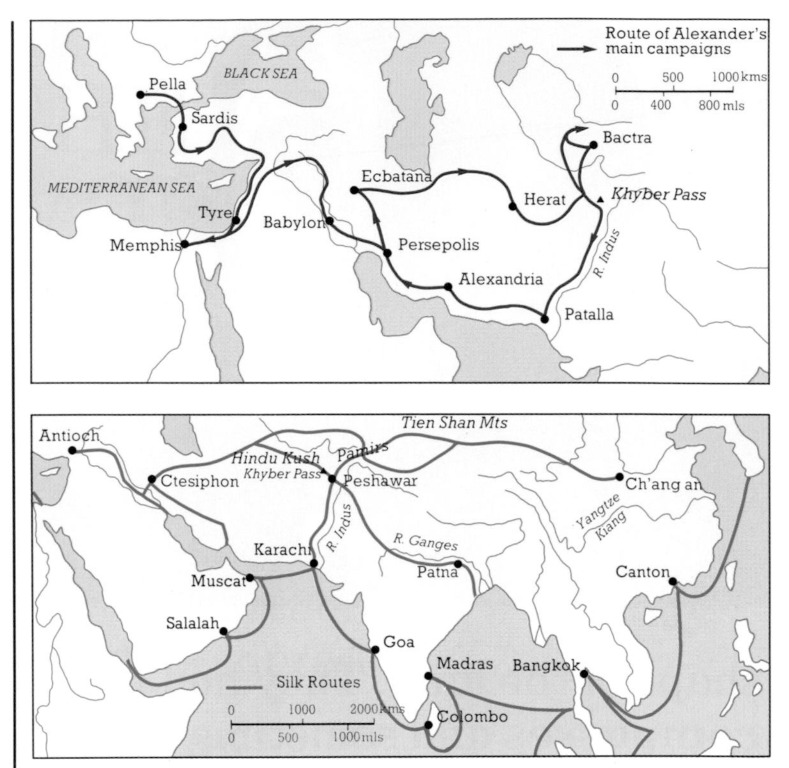

► (Top) Alexander the Great led his conquering army along this route. (Bottom) This map shows the ancient silk trade route across Asia.

▼ Alexander the Great, one of the world's greatest travellers.

The Greeks were the greatest explorers of the ancient world. They set up over 100 **colonies** around the Mediterranean and the Black Sea. About 400 BC, the Greeks began to look beyond the Mediterranean Sea.

Alexander the Great

At the age of 23, Alexander was king of Macedonia – at the time, not part of Greece. He wanted to conquer the whole world, but he had no way of knowing how big it was. In 334 BC, he led his army eastward to conquer Persia – now

Iran – and planned to go on to India. Alexander reached Afghanistan, marched through the Khyber Pass, and went down the Indus river. But he died of a fever at the age of 33, in Babylon, near present-day Baghdad, Iraq.

Exploring the north

Very few Greeks went to explore the damp, cold lands of northern Europe. One of the first to do so was Pytheas. He sailed to England and found out it was an island. He then went farther north to a land he called Thule. Today, we are not sure where Thule is, but it may have been in Norway or Iceland.

The Silk Road

The Chinese wanted to make links with the west, so they could sell silk to the rich people of Europe. No one in Europe knew how to make silk. The Chinese explorer, Chang Chi'en, opened trade routes to the west. Between 138 BC and 126 BC, Chang Chi'en explored the Tien Shan mountains, Pamirs, and Hindu Kush as far west as the Khyber Pass. In AD 399 a Buddhist monk, Fa Hsien, made a 15 year journey as far as Sri Lanka.

▼ Part of the Silk Road in Kirgizia, in southern Soviet Union.

CHAPTER THREE

GROWING NATIONS

The Vikings

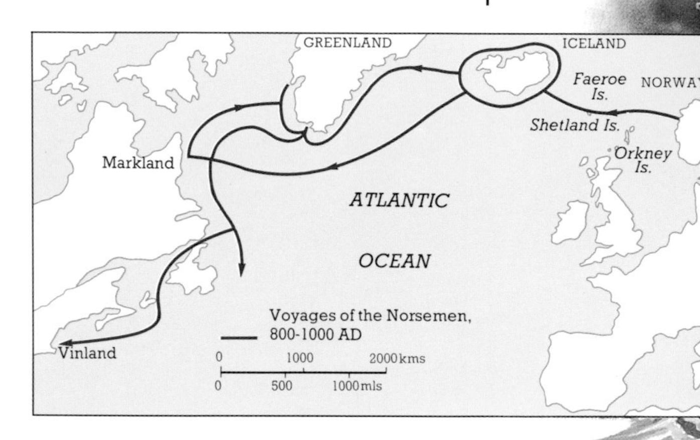

▲ This map shows the routes Vikings took to Vinland in longboats like this one. ▼

Around AD 1000, a brave group of sailors, the Vikings, explored the icy waters of the North Atlantic Ocean. They sailed in sturdy wooden ships called knorrs that held up to 30 people, with food and cattle.

East and west

The Vikings ventured from their home in Scandinavia as far east as Constantinople, which they reached in AD 860. On the way, they went through Russia,

Did you know?

The Vikings, expert sailors, used the wind, the Sun, birds, currents, water colour, ice and fog to navigate.

St Brendan in his currach

moving their ships over land from river to river. About the same time, the Vikings also travelled west to Iceland. One Icelander, Eric the Red, discovered Greenland in AD 982. Many Vikings lived there until the climate became too cold.

Discovering Vinland

About AD 1000, Eric's son, Leif the Lucky, sailed farther west to a warmer, wooded area that he called Vinland. It was in North America. Leif and his men spent a winter there. Two other expeditions followed this one. But the native Indians who lived there attacked the Vikings, making it impossible for them to settle.

Saint Brendan, the Explorer

Saint Brendan may have been the first explorer to cross the Atlantic. After Christianity came to Ireland in AD 432, Irish monks travelled in open boats covered with animal hide, called currachs, looking for islands so they could live simply. Brendan was one of these monks. A book over 1,400 years old tells how Brendan sailed west and found 'crystal columns', that may have been icebergs, and 'a globe of fire', that may have been a volcano. The book also describes beautiful islands to the west, perhaps the Bahamas. No one knows for sure if the story is really true. A modern explorer, Tim Severin, actually sailed across the Atlantic in a currach.

◀ Vikings often stayed home in the winter. In the summer, they travelled great distances to trade or explore.

Going East

Europeans and Asians traded goods for many centuries until the **Mongols** began attacking Europe and the Near East in the 13th century. Then Genghis Khan, their leader, died. Europeans could then travel eastward again. The Pope sent friars – holy men – east to make friends with the Mongols. An Italian friar, John Carpini, was the first European to travel 4,800 km (3,000 miles) to the Mongol capital, in 1245. He wrote about his travels.

Marco Polo

Merchants soon followed the friars east. The most famous merchant traveller was Marco Polo. At the age of 17, he went east to China with his father and uncle. In 1275, the Polos arrived at the court of the **Great Khan**.

Arab explorers

The Arabs were also curious about the world. They travelled by land and sea. Arabs visited the countries of Denmark, England, China, and Russia. The greatest Arabian traveller was Ibn Battuta, from Morocco. In 1325, at the age of 22, Ibn left on a journey that lasted nearly 30 years and covered 120,000 km (75,000 miles)! He explored the Middle East, Russia, India, Africa, and China. Ibn wrote books about his adventures. In one, he described a giant bird, which he called a roc, that could carry away humans! No one knows if this is true however.

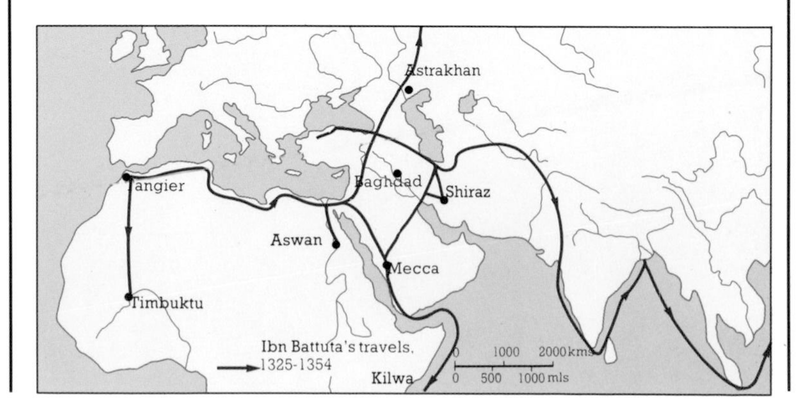

► The journeys of Ibn Battuta in the 1300s.

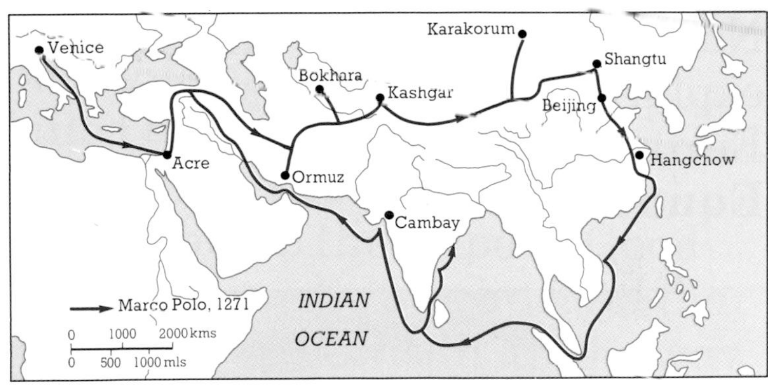

▲ The Great Wall of China – built around 300 BC to keep out invaders.

◀ The routes of Marco Polo's 21 years of travel in China and Asia.

They were impressed by the Khan's palace. The walls were gold and silver and the dining hall could seat 6,000 people! Marco kept a diary of all the things he saw on his travels. He saw a city with 12,000 bridges and he saw huge Chinese ships, called junks. After 21 years of travelling he returned home. For the next 50 years, Europeans freely travelled to the east, until **Muslim** nations would no longer allow them to pass through.

▲ The huge egg of the extinct elephant bird (left) is much bigger than an ostrich egg (centre left), a chicken's egg (centre right) and a tiny hummingbird's egg (right). Ibn Battuta's roc may have been based on the elephant bird.

CHAPTER FOUR

EXPLORING THE PACIFIC

Land of the South

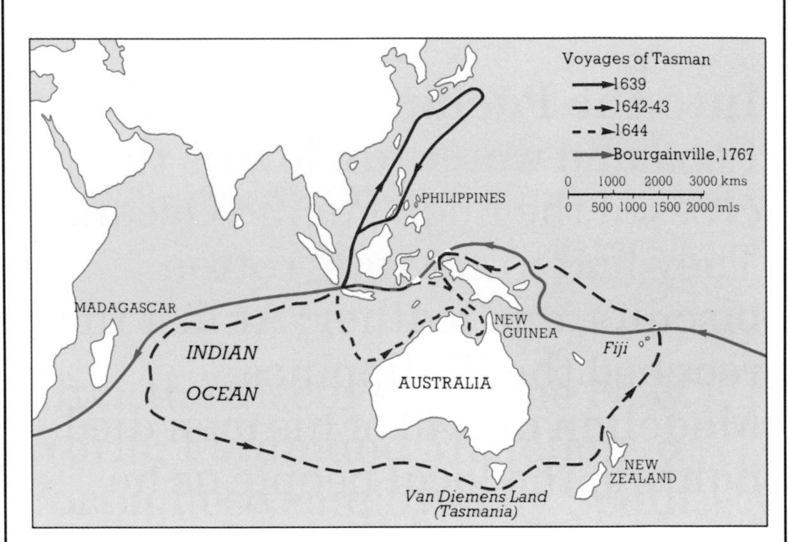

► This map of Australasia shows the routes of the Dutchman Tasman and the Frenchman Bougainville.

In the late 16th century, Europeans believed there was an undiscovered continent in the South Pacific. The Spaniards wanted to find it first. They even named the unseen place Australia, or 'land of the south'.

The Dutch

Willem Jantszoon, a Dutch sailor, first saw Australia in 1606. In 1642, Abel Tasman, another Dutchman, became the first European to sail around Australia. He discovered New

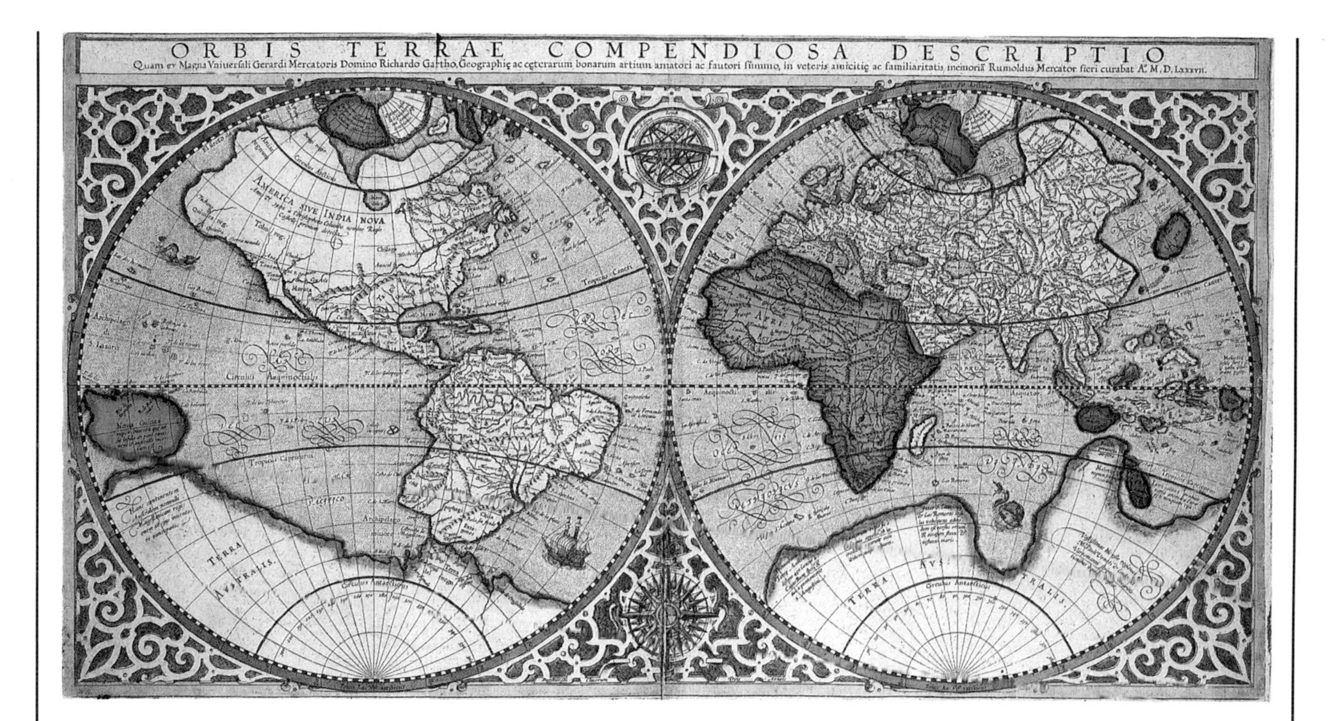

▲ This map of the world drawn in 1595 shows a huge continent that no one had ever seen. Scientists of those days believed that the land was needed there to balance continents in the north.

Zealand, Tasmania, and some other South Pacific islands.

Louis de Bougainville
A French officer, Louis de Bougainville, took scientists along on a Pacific voyage in 1766-69. Many discoveries were made. Jeanne Baré was an expert **botanist** and the first woman to take part in a great voyage of exploration.

◄ When white people first came to Tasmania, they killed many of the Aborigines. Others died from too much drink or disease. These last ones died in the 1860s.

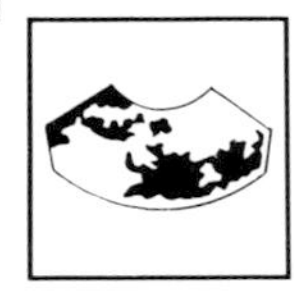

James Cook

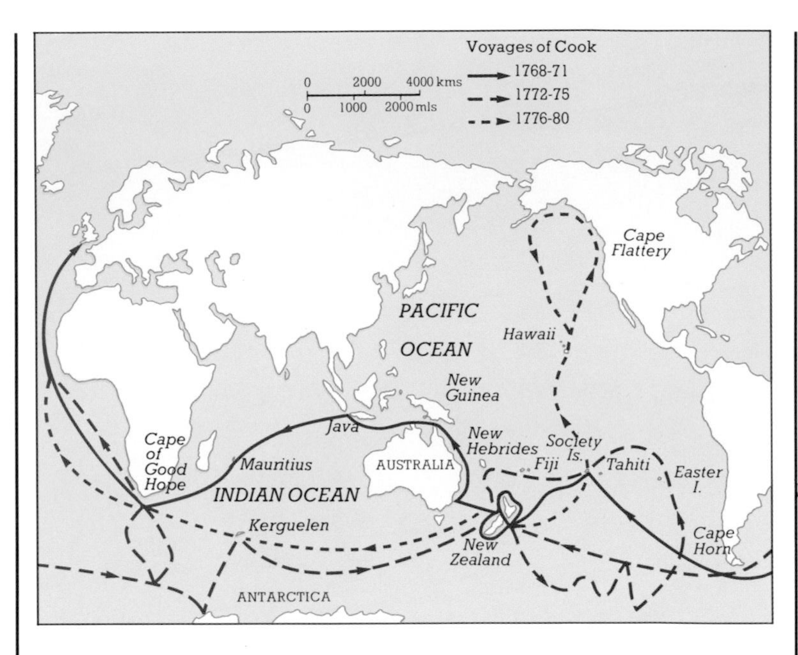

► This map shows the three voyages of Captain Cook.

▲ Cook was a superb sailor and a great leader. He fed his men well to prevent diseases like scurvy.

James Cook, born in 1728, was one of the greatest explorers of the Pacific Ocean. He was a brilliant mathematician and an expert **navigator**. He was interested in making **charts** to show how the planets moved. He also had a secret mission to find a continent south of Australia.

Cook's voyages

Cook made three voyages in the late 1700s. During his first voyage, he drew maps of several islands in the South Pacific, including New Zealand. On his second voyage, he sailed farther south. He did not reach Antarctica, but he did find an icy

◀ Captain Cook's ship, the *Endeavour,* was very strong and measured 30 metres in length.

region of fog and icebergs, where even his sails froze stiff! On his third voyage in 1778, he discovered the Hawaiian Islands. He sailed north through the Bering Strait, searching for a sea route through North America. When ice stopped him, he returned to Hawaii. There, in a fight over a stolen boat, Hawaiians killed him.

Harrison's clock

Englishman John Harrison invented a clock in 1761 that would keep accurate time at sea. For the first time, sailors could find their ship's position east or west. This is called longitude. They compared the local time with the time in England. Cook used Harrison's clock to make accurate maps.

◀ On Cook's second visit to Hawaii, some local people stole one of his boats. When his men tried to get it back, a fight broke out and the Hawaiians killed Cook.

CHAPTER FIVE

ACROSS THE NEW WORLD

The Northwest Passage

▲ Martin Frobisher was a strong Yorkshireman with a bad temper.

While the Spanish were colonizing Central and South America, the British turned their attention to North America. They were convinced that they could find a sea passage around the top of North America that connected the Atlantic and Pacific Oceans. They called it the Northwest Passage.

Sir Martin Frobisher

In 1576, Martin Frobisher was one of the first people to make a serious search for the Northwest Passage. During his search, he and his men were surrounded by **Inuit** warriors in **kayaks**. Five of Frobisher's men disappeared while exploring, so, in anger, he captured an Inuit and took him back to England. Frobisher made three trips in search of the Northwest Passage, but never found it.

◄ Inuit attacked Frobisher's men as they explored Baffin Island.

▼ Frobisher captured this Inuit man and took him back to England.

▼ Polar bears present another danger for Arctic explorers.

Henry Hudson

In 1610, Henry Hudson sailed to North America to find the Northwest Passage. When he reached Canada, Hudson spent the winter with his men in a huge bay, now called Hudson's Bay. Later, his men mutinied. They set him adrift in an open boat, leaving him, his son, and seven companions to die.

Going West

The French explored the inland areas of North America, going by canoe. They traded with the Indians. Jacques Cartier was the first Frenchman to explore Canada. He explored the Gulf of St. Lawrence in 1534 and the St. Lawrence River in the next year.

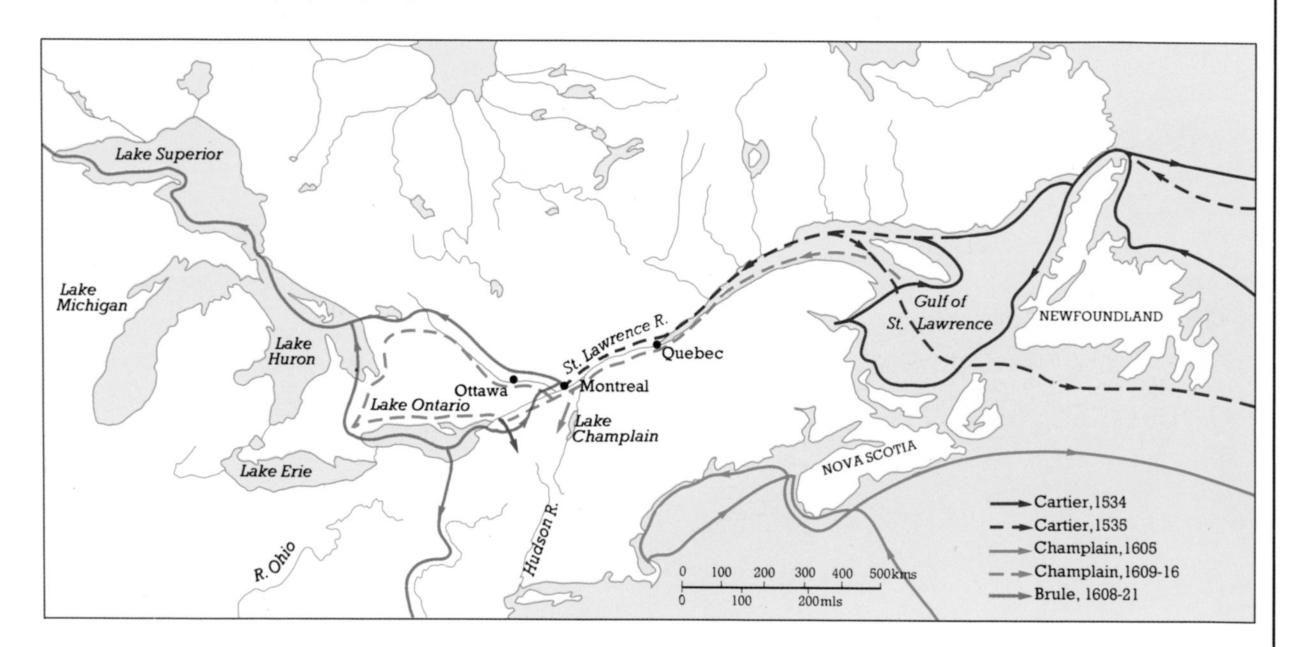

▲ This map shows the routes of the early French explorers in North America.

Later explorers

Sixty years later, Samuel de Champlain, looked for a way across the continent. He explored around Lake Ontario and **founded** a colony in that area. At about the same time, Etienne Brulé explored Lake Ontario, Lake Huron, and Lake Superior. He nearly reached the centre of

the continent. In 1682, Robert de la Salle explored the Mississippi, all the way to the Gulf of Mexico. Alexander MacKenzie, a Scot, explored the great MacKenzie River. He also explored westward from Lake Athabasca. In 1793 he and his men struggled over the Rockies. They were the first to reach the Pacific Ocean overland after a difficult two-month journey.

▲ Early European explorers and settlers traded with the Indians. In exchange for guns, metal tools, and alcoholic drinks, the Indians gave them furs that were valued highly in Europe.

▼ Watched by Indians, Jacques Cartier's 1535 expedition sails westward up the St. Lawrence River.

Breakout from the East

► Frontiersmen lived dangerous lives. They travelled over unknown land and risked being attacked by native Indians and wild animals, like bears.

► Basic items every frontiersman needed to keep warm and safe and for hunting.

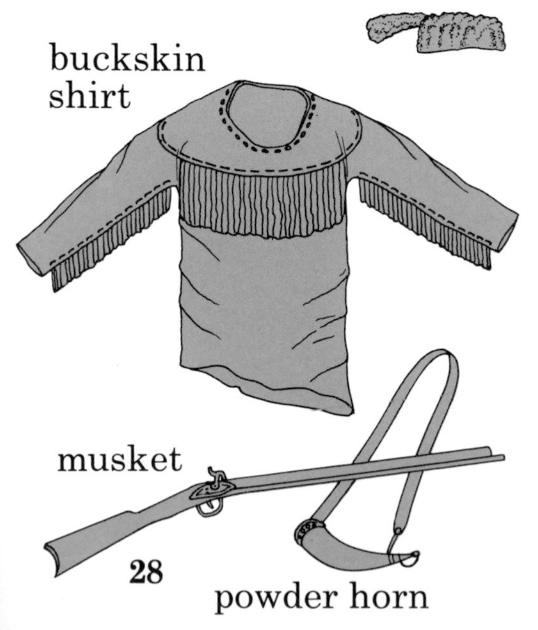

By the mid-1700s, the **settlements** on the east coast were crowded. People began moving west.

Daniel Boone

For a hundred years, men had crossed the Appalachian Mountains to hunt. The best known **frontiersman** was Daniel

Boone. He hunted and explored in Kentucky for years. People began to follow him to find new homes.

Lewis and Clark

In 1803 the US bought a vast

◀ Long lines of wagons rolled along trails found by the first explorers of the American West. This wagon train heads across the prairies into the Rocky Mountains.

stretch of land. It needed to be explored. Meriwether Lewis and William Clark were the leaders of the expedition. They set out in 1804 across the mid-western **prairies**. Soon they were in unknown territory, facing the Rocky Mountains that seemed too high to cross. Fortunately, one member of the expedition was married to a **Shoshoni** Indian woman. She guided them through the mountains, and later saved their lives from Indian warriors.

Lewis and Clark and their men went down the Columbia River to the Pacific. They returned safely the next year. Their **expedition** covered 12,000 kms (7,500 miles) in $2\frac{1}{4}$ years.

▼ A frontiersman from the time of Daniel Boone – between 1750-1800.

The Himalayas

After the Polos, few westerners travelled over the Himalayas to China. In 1661, John Grueber and Albert d'Orville, two **Jesuits**, went to China to set up a European trade route from China to India. They were the first

▲ Mountain climbing became a popular sport in the 19th century.

► The Potala, a great monastery, overlooks the city of Lhasa in Tibet. This was called the Forbidden City because foreigners were not allowed there.

◀ At 8,848 m high, the triangular peak of Everest is the highest in the world (left). But it is almost equalled by other Himalayan giants, like Nuptse (centre) and Lhotse (right).

Europeans to see Lhasa, the capital of Tibet.

Map-making
Travellers usually took regular routes through the Himalayas. But map-makers had to go off these paths. George Everest was the greatest map-maker. Mt. Everest, the world's highest mountain, is named after him.

Did you know?

In 1953, the first men to the top of Mt. Everest were Sir Edmund Hillary and Sherpa Tensing.

Perhaps the greatest explorer of Central Asia was Sven Hedin. He made many journeys and maps of the region. On one journey, between 1894-97, Hedin travelled 19,000 km (12,000 miles) and made 552 pages of maps. Scholars from India, called Pundits, also made maps. Disguised as **pilgrims**, they often explored remote areas.

▲ Sven Hedin, the Swedish explorer, spent most of his life travelling in China and India. He is 70 years old in this picture

Arabian Sands

The Arabs knew their own lands beyond the Red Sea. But the Europeans did not. They had to explore Arabia for themselves.

Mecca

Explorers found it difficult to get to the holy city of **Mecca**. There was a harsh desert to cross and only Muslims were allowed to enter the holy city. In 1500 the first European to see Mecca sneaked in with some pilgrims. In 1762 Danish scientists made the first official exploration of Arabia. Unluckily, all but one

► Muhammad, the Prophet of Islam, was born in Mecca – the holiest city in the Muslim world. At the centre is a square building called the Kaaba. Muslims believe it was built by Abraham. Mecca is closed to non-Muslims.

died of disease. Johann Burckhardt, a Swiss, was more successful. He learned Arabic, dressed like an Arab, and then travelled up the Nile. In 1813 he was the first European to see the great rock temple of Abu Simbel. It had statues 18 m (60 feet) tall. The Arabs thought so well of Burckhardt that they declared him Muslim and allowed him to visit Mecca. In the 19th century, Richard Burton visited Mecca, disguised as an Afghan doctor. During World War I, the Arabs rose up against their Turkish rulers. An Englishman, known as Lawrence of Arabia, fought for the Arabs. He explored the Arabian desert and wrote about what he had found.

▲ (Top) The Empty Quarter of southern Arabia is the world's largest sand desert. (Above) Wilfred Thesiger was the last European to cross the Empty Quarter, in 1948-50. The first was Bertram Thomas, in 1930-31.

CHAPTER SEVEN

SOUTH AMERICA

El Dorado

In the 1500s, the Spaniards went to South America to take as much as gold as possible. For over a hundred years, they stole gold and silver from the Indians.

▼ (Inset) The route of Orellana's expedition down the Amazon. (Below) The Amazon runs through the largest rain forest in the world.

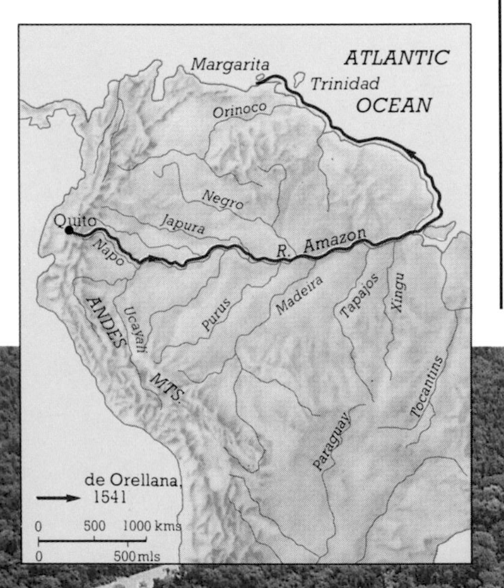

The gilded man

The Spaniards heard about a tribe in Colombia that had an unusual ceremony. Every year, they covered their chief with gold dust that he later washed off in a lake. The Spaniards called this chief El Dorado, meaning 'the gilded man'. Actually, the tribe was small and had little gold.

Exploring the Amazon

After conquering the **Incas** in 1533, the Spaniards began to search for El Dorado. Gonzalo Pizarro and Francisco de Orellana marched 80 men down from the Andes into the **tropical** rain forest. After a month, they could find no food except frogs and snakes. Orellana took 50 men in a boat to search for food. The current swept them down the Amazon river. After fighting hostile tribes, they reached the Atlantic. They travelled almost 5,000 kms and were the first Europeans to cross South America.

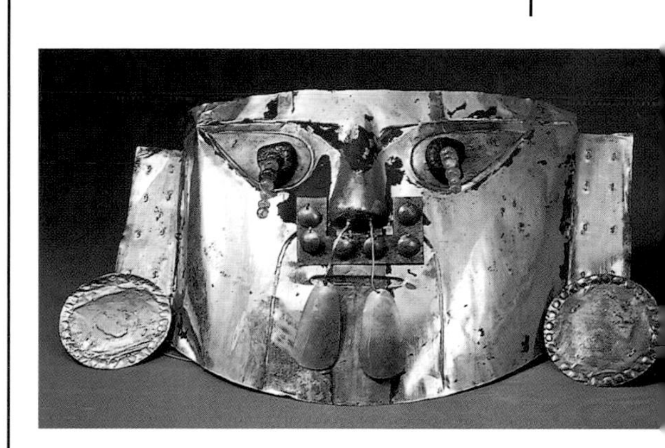

▲ The Incas used gold for ornaments, not for money. This is a gold death mask made in Peru around AD 1200.

▼ Lake Guatavita, in Colombia, where the chief, known as El Dorado, washed gold dust from his body. The Orellana expedition never found the tribe.

Into the Amazon

▼ The Humboldt Current sweeps north from Antarctica.

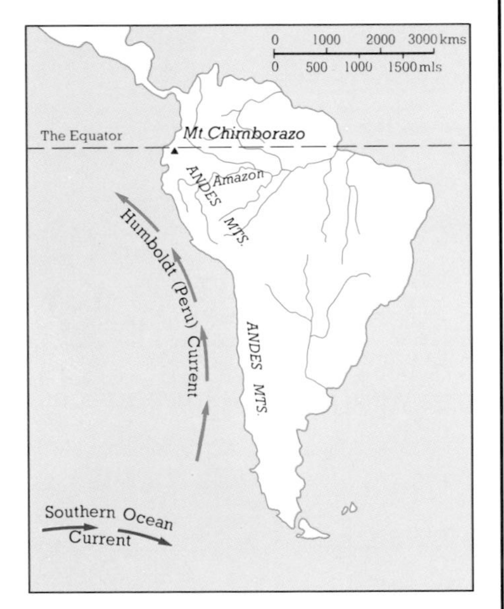

The Amazon basin explorers were mostly scientists. The first, Frenchman Charles-Marie de la Condamine, examined the area in 1743. He found a great number of plants and animals to study in the Amazon region.

Alexander von Humboldt
The greatest scientist-explorer was the German, Alexander von Humboldt. In 1799, he and French botanist Aimé Bonpland followed the Orinoco River. They found many strange creatures – **piranhas**, stingrays, electric eels, and freshwater dolphins. They also saw the Casiquiare Canal, a natural waterway that connects the Orinoco to the Amazon. Later, in the Andes, they climbed the volcano Chimborazo, 6,272 m high. Humboldt was 300 metres

► Chimborazo, a snow-capped volcano in the Andes. Humboldt was the first to climb it in 1802. He reached a height of 5,878 metres, setting a record that was not broken for 30 years.

from the top but the height made him sick. And there was a **ravine** that he could not cross. He had to turn back.

▲ (Above) The explorer-scientist Humboldt (standing) at a camp high in the Andes. (Below) A portrait of Alexander von Humboldt. ▼

The Humboldt Current

Humboldt discovered why there was a desert in Peru. The desert is close to the Equator. Nearby is the Pacific Ocean, where a **current** (the Humboldt current) from Antarctica keeps the water very cold. This mixture of heat on the land and cold in the sea stops rain from falling.

Amazon Life

▲ Henry Bates was attacked by a flock of birds when he captured a toucan for his animal collection.

The Amazon Basin

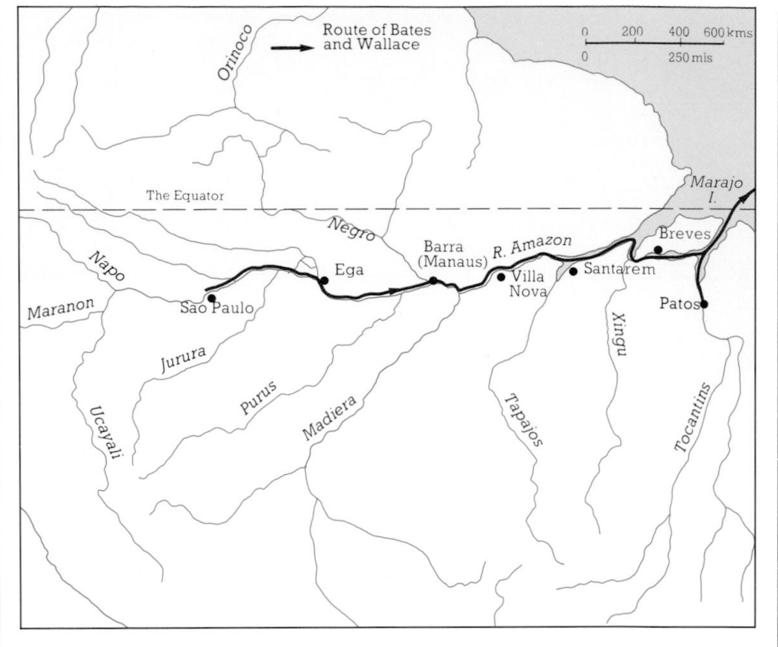

In 1848, Henry Bates and Alfred Wallace, two English scientists, studied Amazon life to learn how different plants and animals **evolved**.

Collecting species

In several years, Bates collected about 14,000 different kinds of insects, over half of them had never been recorded. But Wallace lost his own collection in a fire on the ship. Hamilton Rice, from the US, tried to find the **source** of the Orinoco River, but hostile tribes drove him away. A Brazilian, Candido Rondon, made many trips to meet Indian tribes. He once travelled with former US

▲ Wildlife of the Amazon.

President Theodore Roosevelt. Roosevelt said the Amazon was a 'green hell'.

Mapping the Amazon

The best known Amazon explorer was Percy Fawcett. For years he made maps of new areas. In 1925, he and his son went to search for an ancient lost city. They vanished without a trace. Indians probably killed them.

▼ Col. Percy Fawcett and his son disappeared in the Amazon in 1925.

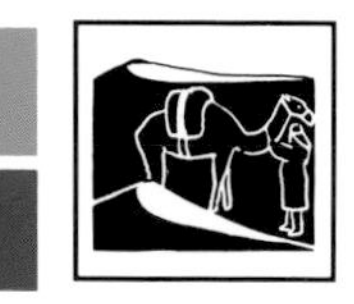

CHAPTER EIGHT

AFRICA

The Sahara

At the end of the 18th century, the inland areas of Africa were still unknown to Europeans. British explorers went there to look for wealth, scientific information, and new lands. First they wanted to find Timbuktu, visited 400 years earlier by Ibn Battuta. They also wanted to find where the River Niger began.

The River Niger

In 1795, Mungo Park, a 24-year-old Scottish doctor, set out to map

Timbuktu

In 1824, a British Major, Alexander Laing, set out to find Timbuktu. It took him over a year, and Tuareg tribesmen nearly killed him. Laing was the first European to cross the Sahara Desert from north to south and enter Timbuktu. He never lived to describe this famous city. His guide killed him soon after he left it. René Caillie, a Frenchman, was the first European to describe Timbuktu. He reached the city in 1828.

▼ Mungo Park mapped the River Niger.

the River Niger. He survived many adventures, including four months in prison. He travelled 500 kms (300 miles) and discovered that the Niger flowed east. In 1805, he returned with 40 Europeans to find where it ran out into the sea. They set out from the River Gambia, but only a few lived to reach the Niger. The rest, including Park, died before reaching the river's mouth.

In 1822, three men travelled to Africa's Lake Chad. They were the first Europeans to see it. One man died, but Dixon Denham and Hugh Clapperton brought back amazing reports of African kingdoms south of the Sahara.

▲ Timbuktu, once a rich trade city, is on the southern edge of the Sahara Desert. The Tuareg, like the man below, and the Arabs have been trading here for centuries.

The Nile

► This map shows three expeditions to find the source of the Nile.

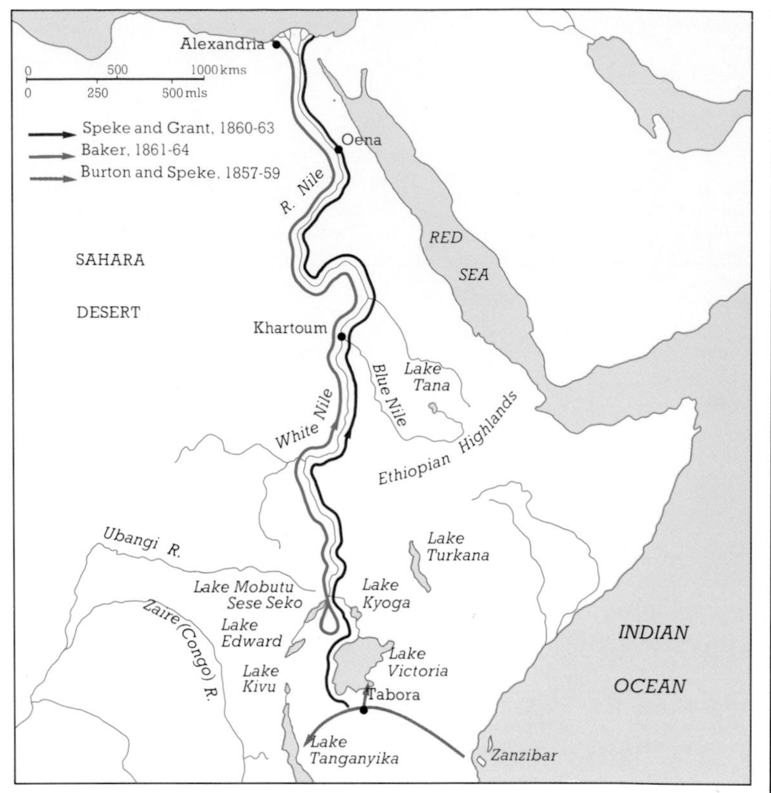

▲ Richard Burton once disguised himself as an Afghan, so he could enter Mecca, the holiest Muslim city.

By the mid-19th century, people still did not know where the source of the River Nile was. It seemed such a mystery. Some said it rose between 'the Mountains of the Moon'. The British Royal Geographical Society sent an expedition in 1856. The leader was Richard Burton. He was an army officer who could speak 25 different languages.

Lake Victoria

In 1857, Burton and John Speke, discovered Lake Tanganyika. Both men became sick, but Speke was strong enough to go on. He

travelled north to find a great lake, Lake Victoria. Speke was sure this was the Nile's source. He returned home ahead of Burton and broke the news. Speke soon organized another expedition, and James Grant joined him. They found where one branch of the Nile flows out of Lake Victoria. They missed finding out that the river also flowed through Lake Albert. Later, they met Samuel Baker and his wife. They were also searching for the Nile's source. The Bakers reached Lake Albert and Murchison Falls in 1864.

▲ The Murchison Falls, where the River Nile flows out of Lake Albert.

▼ Up until the 19th century people believed that the source of the River Nile lay somewhere near Mount Kilimanjaro in Tanzania.

Missionary Explorers

► David Livingstone and Henry Morton Stanley explored and mapped much of central Africa.

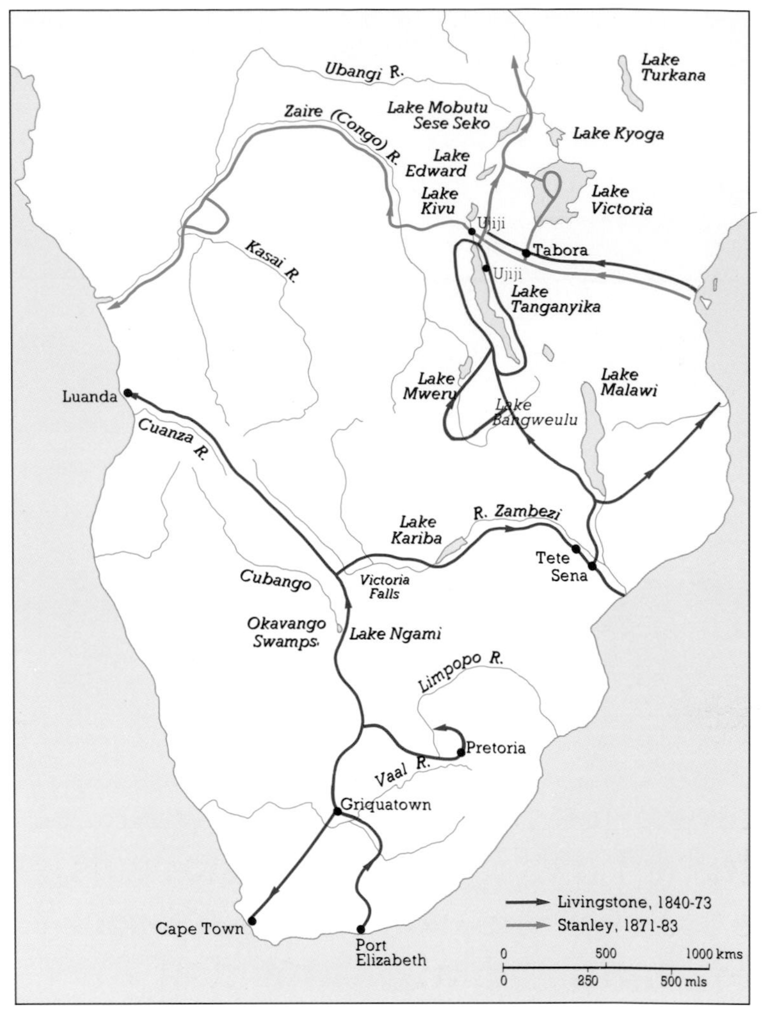

▼ Livingstone explored the River Zambezi in 1855-56. He reported that it was calm. But at that time he had not seen the fierce Quebrabasa rapids.

David Livingstone is a very famous explorer. In 1841 he went to South Africa as a **missionary**. He was one of the first to cross the Kalahari desert. He found Lake Ngami. Next, he crossed Africa from coast to coast, searching for a good trade route. In 1858, he led a British expedition up the Zambezi River, but dangerous **rapids** blocked his way. Later, in 1866, he began searching for the sources of the Nile and Congo rivers. He ran out of money and supplies, and fell ill on the shore of Lake Tanganyika. When he did not return, people thought he was lost or dead.

Henry Morton Stanley

Just then Henry Morton Stanley, a US news reporter, arrived with supplies. Stanley spoke those famous words, 'Dr. Livingstone, I presume?' Livingstone recovered and went on trying to find the 'mountains of the moon'. In 1873 he fell ill again and died. Stanley led several more expeditions. He explored more of central Africa by travelling along the River Congo.

▼ Sailing up the Zambezi in his boat, Livingstone found the dangerous rapids he missed earlier.

▼ On a later expedition, Livingstone fell ill. His food and medicine had been stolen. Just in time, Stanley reached him with fresh supplies.

CHAPTER NINE

INLAND AUSTRALIA

Across the Divide

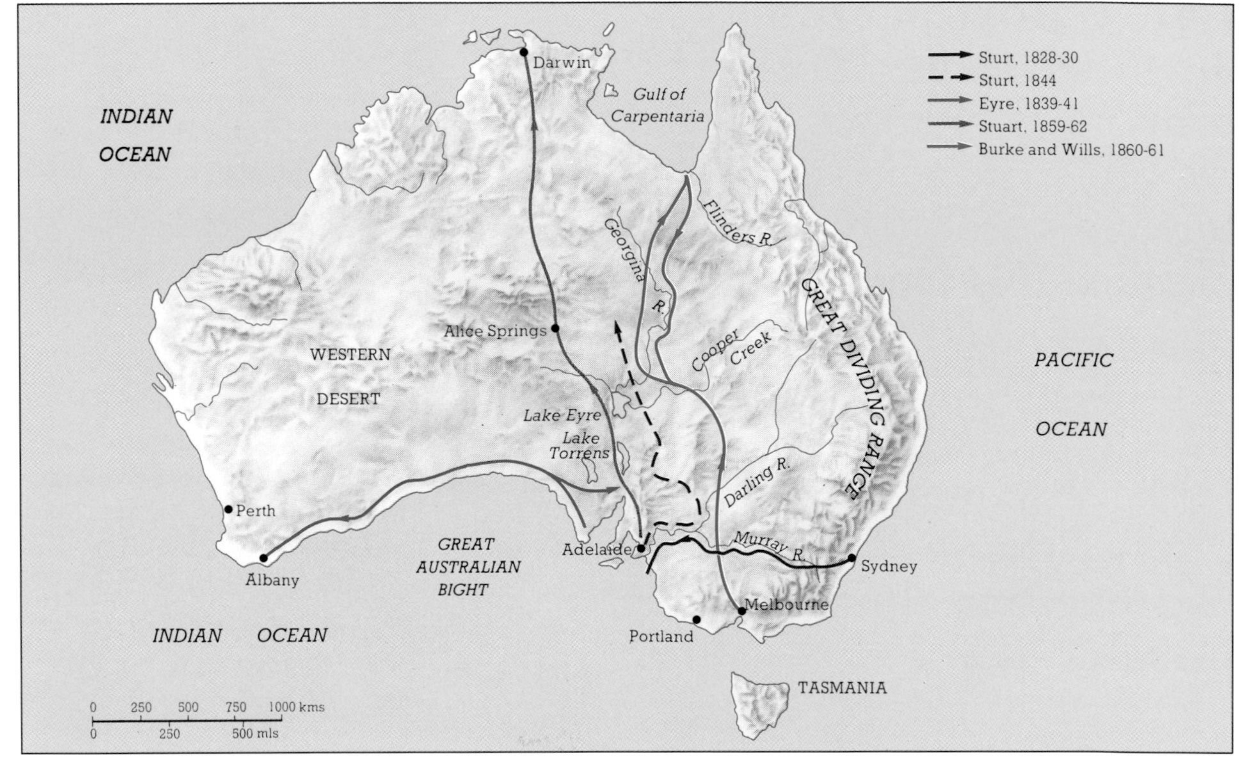

▲ The routes of the main explorers of Australia's outback, or inland.

For **decades** after the British first settled in Australia, few crossed the Great Dividing Range of mountains along the eastern shore. Only the Aborigines lived in the outback – inland Australia.

Mapping inland

In 1829, Charles Sturt and six others explored down the

Murrumbidgee and Murray rivers to the southern coast. Then they rowed back against the current for nearly 1,600 km (1,000 miles). They made reports of good land and many people started moving west. About ten years later, Edward Eyre left Adelaide

to explore northward. When he reached desert areas, he turned west instead. He found that in 1,600 kms (1,000 miles) of the south desert coast there were no rivers. Two guides killed his companion and stole the supplies. Eyre and one faithful Aborigine, Wylie, came across a French ship and were given food. They went on until they reached Albany.

▲ The Darling River and others like it helped explorers reach inland Australia.

◀ These cliffs in the Great Dividing Range, 150 metres high, show why it was a major barrier to explorers.

▼ Edward Eyre and the Aborigine, Wylie, survived the 1840 exploration of the south coast.

The Simpson Desert

Charles Sturt believed there was an inland lake in Australia. In 1844 he led an expedition to find it. The men spent months in desert country. Then they entered the Simpson Desert, a huge wasteland of red rock and sand. Sturt turned back.

The Telegraph Race

In 1859, the government of Australia decided to link north and south by **telegraph**. It offered a prize of £2,500 to the first person who could make the crossing. Two rival teams set out. John Stuart led one team. They went farther north than any European had gone before. They passed Alice Springs and a

► Charles Sturt starting off on his journey of 1844. He hoped to find a great inland sea, but found only seas of grass, and sand and rock.

▼ Robert Burke was brave, but his bad temper made him unpopular.

mountain that was later named after Stuart. When he ran out of food, he had to turn back. He was only 500 kms (300 miles) from the north coast. Two years later, he made it all the way. Robert Burke led the second team, using camels to help them. He split his men into two groups, one to wait for supplies to catch up, the other to hurry north. Burke and William Wills made a final dash and completed the crossing from south to north. They had planned to meet up with the others back at Cooper's Creek. But they could not find each other. All died of starvation but John King — a walking skeleton kept alive by Aborigines.

▲ Cooper's Creek was the meeting place for Burke and his men. Most of them died in the deserts near here.

▼ Here is a camel caravan like the one Burke used for his expedition. He was the first to bring these animals into Australia. Camels travel better in deserts than horses.

The North

CHAPTER TEN

THE ENDS OF THE EARTH

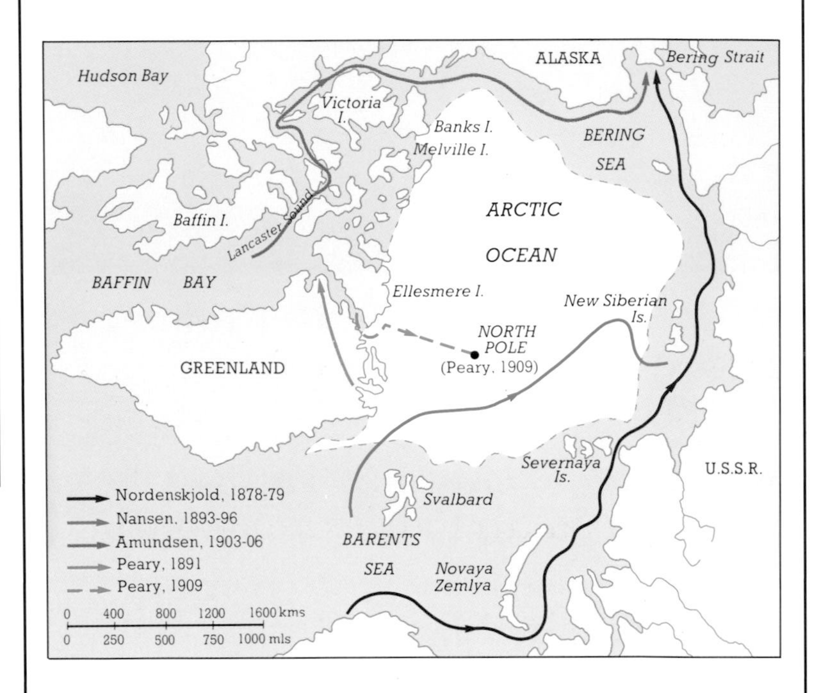

▶ This map shows the routes of the major Arctic expeditions.

First to the Pole

Robert Peary of the United States was the first person to reach the North Pole in 1909.

▼ An Inuit family, dressed warmly to survive the severe cold of the far north.

For centuries, people have wondered about the remote icy regions of the far north. In the 19th century, several British explorers travelled north of Canada. They could not find the Northwest Passage that would connect the Pacific and Atlantic oceans.

Discovering Magnetic North

In 1829, John Ross led the Arctic

◀ Wally Herbert and his men were the first to cross the polar ice cap.

expedition that found the **Magnetic North Pole**. He had to abandon his damaged ship and live in a small makeshift house during the Arctic winter. Luckily, a whaling ship rescued them. Sir John Franklin led a less fortunate expedition in 1845. His ship became frozen in ice and he died. Some of his men tried to walk away on the ice, but they too met with a chilly death. Baron Nils Nordenskjold, a Swedish explorer, travelled north of Siberia and found the Northeast Passage in 1878-79. The Northwest Passage was finally navigated in 1903-06 by Roald Amundsen, from Norway.

Nansen

Nansen Fridtjof Nansen from Norway designed a ship that would slip up out of the water when ice closed in. In 1893, after sailing north, Nansen let his ship freeze in. He then went on with sleds and kayaks. Nansen came within 386 kms (240 miles) of the Pole.

▼ Fridtjof Nansen was a great explorer and a brilliant scentist. He also drew fine illustrations of his travels.

The South

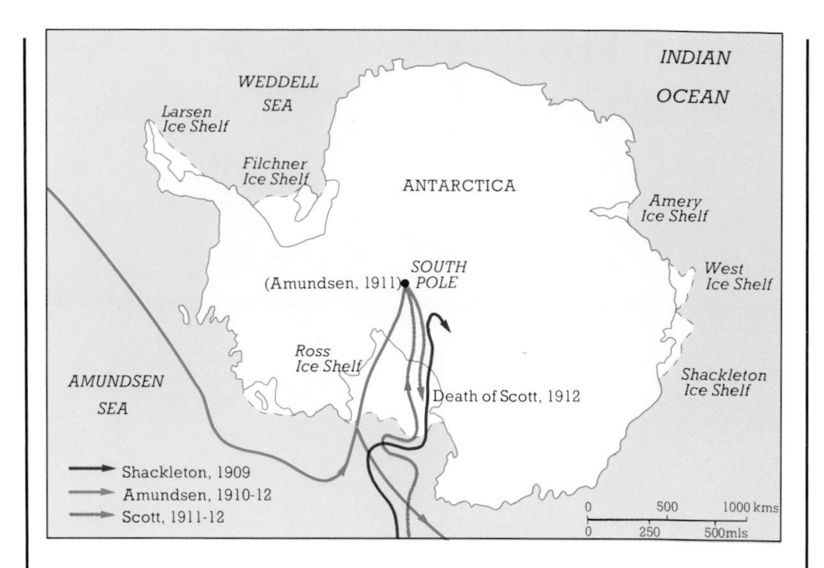

▶ The main routes in search of the South Pole.

▲ Robert Scott writes in his diary before setting out for the South Pole.

Antarctica was the last continent to be explored. Explorers raced to be first to the South Pole.

The Race to the South Pole
In 1908 Ernest Shackleton, a British explorer, discovered the Beardmore Glacier. He almost

▶ In the Antarctic, high winds whip the snow into a fog-like, blinding white out. Bare flesh can freeze in less than a minute.

reached the South Pole. Just 160 kms (100 miles) from the pole he ran short of food and had to turn back. In 1911, two men raced for the pole. Roald Amundsen, a Norwegian, used Arctic sledge dogs called huskies. British expedition leader Robert Scott had ponies and motorized sledges. The sledges soon broke down. The ponies could not survive the cold. For four weeks, Scott and his men hauled their supplies on foot. Then Scott took four men and hurried the remaining 286 kms (178 miles) to the pole. When they arrived they found Amundsen had been there 34 days earlier, on 14 December, 1911. With his dogs, he had made the trip in seven weeks. Scott and his four men died on the return journey.

▲ The Beardmore Glacier.

▼ Here is Shackleton's well-stocked base hut.

The bitter end

From the South Pole, Scott and his men started back to their base camp, 300 kms (200 miles) away. They were running out of food and were exhausted. One died on the Beardmore Glacier. Another man aware that food was running out, wandered away. The other three died 12 days later, only 18 kms (11 miles) from food and shelter.

◀ The Norwegian flag is raised over the South Pole.

The Last Unknown

▶ Ernest Shackleton had his ship, *Endurance,* locked in ice for nine months, and then it sank.

▼ The type of clothing modern explorers need to survive in the Arctic and Antarctic.

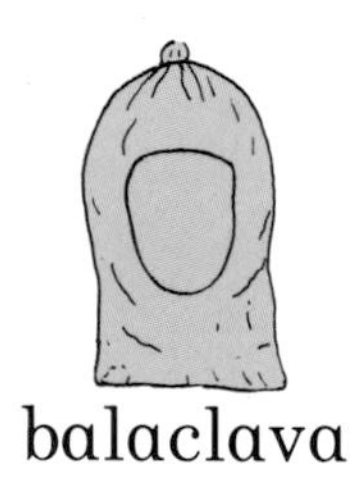

balaclava

padded snow jacket

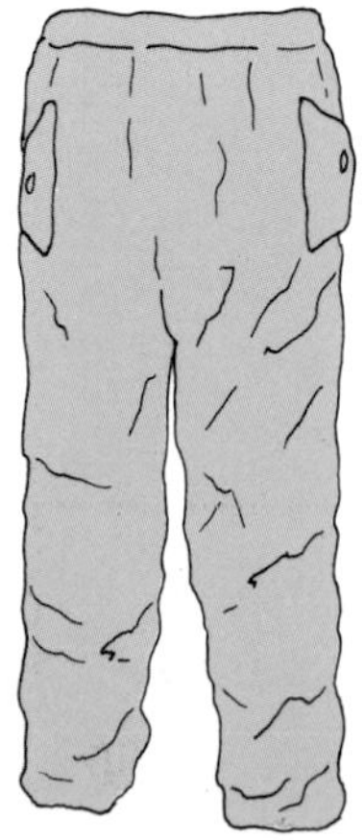

padded over-trousers

lined gloves

snow boots

In 1915, Ernest Shackleton made one of the most heroic journeys in Antarctica. His ship froze in the ice and later sank. He and his 28 crewmen camped for four months on the ice until it broke up. They rowed to a small island. Then Shackleton and five men sailed in a small boat 1,400 kms (870 miles) to an island whaling station for help. All of his men were saved.

Mapping and photographing
Today, our interest in Antarctica

is scientific. In 1946, the US sent a crew to map and photograph over half the coast. In 1957, a British team crossed Antarctica in snow-mobiles. They found that the **icecap** averages 2.5 kms (1.5 miles) thick. If it melted, it would be as much water as the Atlantic Ocean!

The 12 Nation Treaty

In 1959, 12 nations signed a treaty, promising not to claim any more Antarctic land and to use the area only for peaceful research.

▲ Ice-breakers like this make modern Antarctic research safer.